D0761894

Gearhead Garage

SPORT BIKES

PETER BODENSTEINER

BLACK
RABBIT
BOOKS

Bolt is published by Black Rabbit Books
P.O. Box 3263, Mankato, Minnesota, 56002.
www.blackrabbitbooks.com
Copyright © 2017 Black Rabbit Books

Design and Production by Michael Sellner
Photo Research by Rhonda Milbrett

Library of Congress Control Number: 2015954671

HC ISBN: 978-1-68072-034-1   PB ISBN: 978-1-68072-261-1

Printed in the United States at CG Book Printers,
North Mankato, Minnesota, 56003. PO #1790 4/16

Web addresses included in this book were working and appropriate
at the time of publication. The publisher is not responsible for broken
or changed links.

Image Credits
Adobe Stock: sergio37_120, 4–5;
Alamy: dpa picture alliance archive, 14–
15; imageBROKER, 31; Manor Photography,
12; Peter Brogden, 14; ZUMA Press, Inc., Back
Cover, 1, 26; desktopwallpapers4.me: SCHVENIN-
GEN, 9; Dreamstime: Daveh900, 32; Supertrooper,
18–19; Flickr: Bernie Lampert, 11; BTO Sports, 9; Ver-
onica Woods, 8; Getty: Thananuwat Srirasant / Stringer,
17; getwallpapers.pw, 25; nikonites.com: FotoJack, 22–23;
Shutterstock: Castleski, 28; easaab, 27; enciktat, Cover;
Gines Romero, 23; Handatko, 8; Ivan Garcia, 7; Johannes
Kornelius, 22–23; Ken Tannenbaum, 29; Sergey Kohl, 28;
Tereshchenko Dmitry, 22; VanderWolf Images, 20; Ve-
ronikaMaskova, 28–29; Wikipedia: Badass, 20; Dennis
Bratland, 3; Greg Knapp, 20
Every effort has been made to contact copyright
holders for material reproduced in this
book. Any omissions will be rectified in
subsequent printings if notice is
given to the publisher.

BOLT

CONTENTS

CHAPTER 1

Famously Fast

The rider bends low over the handlebars. She tucks behind the bike's windscreen. A twist of the **handgrip** feeds fuel to the **engine**. The sport bike blasts down the highway. Soon, it's just a streak in the distance.

Sporty and Speedy

Sport bikes are built for speed. These motorcycles are small and light. They have fat, sticky tires. And their engines kick out tons of power. These bikes go fast.

Sport bikes look like racing bikes. Many people do race these motorcycles. But sport bikes can be driven on city streets too.

By the Numbers

77 MILES (124 KILOMETERS)

DISTANCE THE HONDA CBR250R
CAN GO PER GALLON OF FUEL

AROUND
450
POUNDS
(204 kilograms)

WEIGHT OF A
SPORT BIKE

$184,000

COST OF A
2016 HONDA
RC213V-S

186 MILES
(299 KM) PER HOUR
TOP SPEED OF A
SUZUKI HAYABUSA

CHAPTER 2

The History of Sport Bikes

The history of sport bikes goes back to the 1960s. At that time, drivers sped café racers in road races. These bikes looked a lot like regular motorcycles.

Then came the 1969 Honda CB750. The bike had a four-**cylinder** engine. It was fast and smooth. And it was also **affordable**. Many people say the CB750 is the first modern sport bike.

Colorful Racers

During the 1980s, sport bikes got colorful. Companies put plastic covers called **fairings** on the bikes. Fairings helped the bikes slip through the air.

People painted the plastic bold colors. The colorful look made sport bikes stand out.

SPORT BIKES VS. RACE CARS

Every year, sport bikes get faster and more advanced. Today's bikes can even compete with race cars.

TIME TO GO FROM
0 to 60 MILES
(97 KM) PER HOUR

Lexus LFA

TIME TO GO FROM
0 to 60 MILES
(97 KM) PER HOUR

3.7 SECONDS

TOP SPEED
202 MPH
(325 KPH)

PRICE
$375,000

TOP SPEED
185 MPH
(298 KPH)

PRICE
$13,990

CHAPTER 3

Tuned Up

Sport bikes have a **unique** look. Riders lean over the front tires. The bikes are built like this on purpose. Putting more weight on the front tire improves **handling**.

The two tires aren't far apart on sport bikes either. This spacing makes it easy to change direction quickly.

HEIGHT
44.9 INCHES
(114 cm)

LENGTH 80.8 INCHES (205 cm)

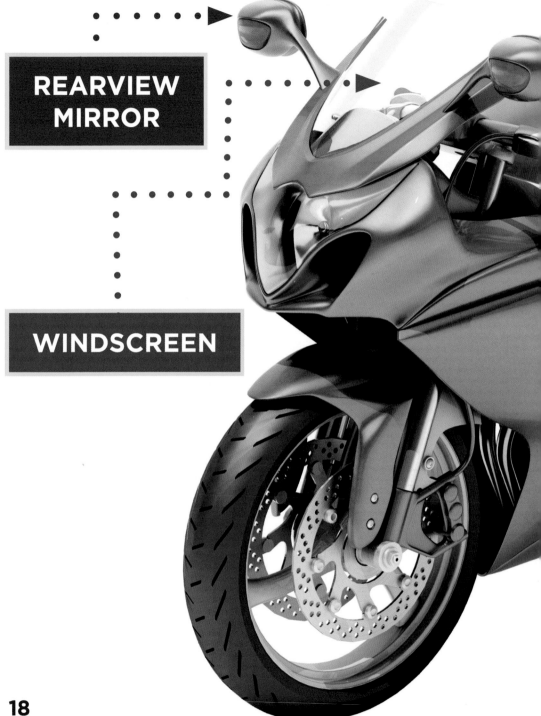

REARVIEW MIRROR

WINDSCREEN

FUEL TANK

FAIRING

HANDLEBARS

SUPERBIKE

MIDDLEWEIGHT

LIGHTWEIGHT

20

Engines

There are three classes of sport bikes. They are divided by the sizes of engines they have. Superbikes have the most powerful engines. They are great for racing. Middleweights have smaller engines. But they can still race. Lightweights have the smallest engines. They are best for fun, easy rides.

Stunt Riding

stoppies

standing the bike on the front wheel

wheelies
standing the bike on the back wheel

christs

CHAPTER 4

The Future of Sport Bikes

People change motorcycles to fit their needs. Some people are starting to take off the fairings. These "naked bikes" could be the future of sport bikes.

Future sport bikes might be more comfortable too. Some people want sport bikes they can use on long-distance rides.

Always Going Faster

Companies will add new technology to sport bikes too. Computers might help control bikes. Electric motors might become popular too.

But one thing will stay the same. Sport bikes will always be

electric motor

1969

Honda CB750 is released.

1970s

Companies work to improve sport bike braking systems.

1945

World War II ends.

1945

The first people walk on the moon.

1969

1980s

Sport bikes begin to look almost exactly like racing motorcycles.

1990s

Bike makers start to create naked bikes.

2016

The Mount St. Helens volcano erupts.

1980

2001

Terrorists attack the World Trade Center and Pentagon.

affordable (uh-FORD-uh-bul)—not too expensive

cylinder (SIL-en-dur)—a part of an engine

engine (EN-jin)—a machine that changes energy into mechanical motion

fairing (FAHR-ing)—a part of a structure that makes a smooth outline and reduces drag

handgrip (HAND-gryp)—a handle

handling (HAND-ling)—the way a car, motorcycle, or other vehicle drives

unique (yoo-NEEK)—very special or unusual

BOOKS

David, Jack. *Sport Bikes.* Motorcycles. Bellwether Media, 2008.

Mason, Paul. *Motorcycles.* Motorsports. Mankato, MN: Amicus, 2011.

Woods, Bob. *Smokin' Motorcycles.* Fast Wheels! Berkeley Heights, NJ: Enslow Publishers, Inc., 2013.

WEBSITES

A Brief History of Motorcycling
www.nhtsa.gov/people/injury/pedbimot/ motorcycle/00-NHT-212-motorcycle/history5-6.html

Motorcycle Types
www.americanmotorcyclist.com/riding/street/ gettingstarted/motorcycletypes.aspx

INDEX